201
Questions
to Ask Your
Kids

Pepper Schwartz, Ph.D.

AVON BOOKS  NEW YORK

201 Questions to Ask Your Kids/Parents is a game developed to spark meaningful conversation between parents and children. It is not meant as a substitute to family counseling or individual therapy. Always consult a professional therapist to resolve serious emotional or behavioral problems.

AVON BOOKS, INC.
An Imprint of HarperCollins*Publishers*
10 East 53rd Street
New York, New York 10022-5299

 A becker&mayer! book, Kirkland, Washington
www.beckermayer.com

Copyright © 2000 by Pepper Schwartz, Ph.D.
Published by arrangement with the author
Library of Congress Catalog Card Number: 99–96539
ISBN: 0-380-80525-1
www.harpercollins.com

First Avon Books Trade Paperback Printing: February 2000

AVON TRADEMARK REG. U.S. PAT. OFF. AND IN OTHER COUNTRIES, MARCA REGISTRADA, HECHO EN U.S.A.

Printed in the U.S.A.

OPM 10 9 8 7 6 5 4 3 2 1

••

To my children,

Cooper Schwartz Skolnik and Ryder Schwartz Skolnik,

for all their help on this book

and for sharing their thoughts and their lives with me.

I love you very much.

••

AN INTRODUCTION FOR PARENTS

"What happened today at school?"

"Nothing."

"How was the movie?"

"Good."

Yuck! Is this bonding? Is this intimacy? Is this even news? Surely this isn't the kind of communication we fantasized about when we first decided to have children. *No*, we thought about all those late-night talks we would have over hot chocolate, musing about school or friends or—whatever. And maybe, from time to time, we do have a heartfelt conversation that feels like we are really getting hold of our children's day to day lives—even their inner feelings.

But most of the time it's frustrating because we know that we are missing so much good stuff. We want to know more about their random thoughts, their hopes, their preferences, their perspective, their disappointments, what they are learning about life. We want to know them better. We want to know them the best we can.

And guess what? Our children are missing some of the good stuff about us, too. Most of the time, parents are the ones who start the conversations and set the terms for discussion. And some of the things that kids might be interested in never surface. Sometimes because parents introduce subjects that are interesting to themselves, they forget that there are all kinds of other questions that are primarily interesting to kids. So if parents are the only ones who get to select the topics of the day—it's boring. Or it's threatening—like questions about how school went today, or how did you do on your test? Or open-ended questions like "Whatever happened to that friend of yours, Jimmy?"

Kids sometimes don't like these kinds of questions because they think of them as unsafe territory—where is this kind of questioning going to lead? Am

I going to get a lecture ? Are we just sentences away from turning from a casual mention of my friend into the usual warnings about not spending too much time away from my homework? Kids often shy away from conversation because (a) it means trouble, not fun; (b) it's not about some-thing they really care about; or (c) the questions are too broad, too hard for them to organize into any easy, focused answer. Result? Monosyllabic answers and very short conversations.

A Better Idea

It's not hard to think of a better idea than badger-ing your child to distraction, trying to extract some kind of information. The premise of this book is that communication can actually be fun for both parties—if it's seen as playful, occasionally sus-penseful and surprising (in a good way), and if both parties (parent and child) are on equal footing. "Equal footing" means mutual control over the con-versation so that the child, as well as the parent, gets to ask some of the questions he or she wants to ask, and everybody gets an equal chance to hold forth and be in the spotlight. No one interrupts the speaker, everyone gets an equal opportunity to ask a question, and each person gets to ask the question he or she is interested in having answered.

It might not seem very radical to say that in this "game" each person gets some uninterrupted time to answer a question and each person gets a chance to ask something that he or she thinks is really interesting, but the truth is, it doesn't happen with any regularity in most households. Several studies have found that there are fewer than twenty minutes a day of conversation between parents and children if you subtract talking that has to do with a command or criticism. There is also a lot of evidence that interruption is common—and usually done by the person with the most power. So guess how kids experience conversation: however it's begun, the parent often doesn't let the kid finish the thought (or complaint).

But this time, we aren't going to let each side fall into their old habits. Because this time it's a game—and in games, we follow the rules. And the rules here are to listen, to have a chance to get your thoughts across, and to answer honestly without being cut off.

To differentiate this game from other conversation (and, I hope, to set a model eventually for other conversation) the game begins at a certain time. I suggest either during dinner—especially if you are sick and tired of silent meals punctuated only by the television or lectures that you personally deliver—or after dinner, when the homework is finished and it's almost lights out. Car trips are good, too, if you, the driver, can tolerate thinking and driving at the same time. But, to begin this game in the right spirit, ask your kids when they would like to play it—give them the choice of during dinner, after dinner, in the car next Sunday, or some other time you suggest. Remember, for a lot of kids, totally open-ended questions are yucky.

Getting Kids Interested

The questions in this book are organized around a lot of topics that kids want to know about—often about you. They are also organized around questions that help you and your children to be intro-spective. A little navel gazing isn't bad—adults pay psychologists a high fee to help them do it, so it's fun and inexpensive to do it this way, not in crisis, just exploring. Kids want to know you—the real you, the sometimes-imperfect you—and this helps them get backstage, behind the parent perform-ance you find yourself doing despite your desire to do the contrary.

And because disclosure invites reciprocity, your openness will encourage their openness and their interest. At the end of these conversations you should all feel you know each other—and your-selves—a little better. This is a lot of fun. So once you do this, you will all want to do it again (provid-ed you don't let the game go on too long). How-ever, there is always the issue of getting kids interested enough to *try* it. So here is the way to get them intrigued: turn to the first page of ques-tions that kids can ask parents.

Ask if any of those sound interesting. I think at least one of them will sound enticing, except perhaps for very young children. (This book works best for kids in middle school and older, but some younger kids are so with it that they will have no problem at all getting into the spirit of asking questions. We've had five-year-olds ask and answer some of these questions as If they were on a T.V. game show.) Then show your kids some of the questions that you could ask them—a lot of them will be questions that they will want to answer: questions about their favorite music, why they like (or don't like) heavy metal bands, the three most disgusting foods they have eaten at home, etc. Wouldn't you have liked to tell your parents the answer to "What meal would you prefer never to have again?" (assuming, of course, they could be good sports about it)?

If you promise that you'll only play for half an hour (or less, depending on your kids), most kids will be open to trying the game. You can always re-up for another half an hour if everyone still wants to keep going. Just lay out the rules right at the beginning—and make sure everyone agrees. They are:

1. No answer is stupid. No grimacing, eye rolling, or in any way laughing at someone unless they are saying something funny.

2. Everyone gets to answer without interruption. Follow-up questions are allowed ("But I thought you *liked* beets!"), but follow-up answers aren't *required*. "Nope" will suffice (as an answer to the follow-up). However, if the person wants, they can do a whole riff on the history of beet hating—you asked, after all.

3. Questions that hit a recent sore spot should be avoided if at all possible. For example, if your child has just missed making the team or been dumped by a major heartthrob, you might want to avoid those kinds of questions the first couple of times you play the game (unless you think he or she wants to talk about love and its disappointments).

4. Everyone is, in fact, allowed to avoid *two* questions per game—more if they really insist upon it. This has to be fun, remember? We want kids to *insist* that time gets saved before bedtime to play 201—so better to lose one answer than to lose their interest and confidence in the whole game.

What If You Really Want to Hear More About Something That Interests You?

There is always another time, sometimes a better time for a really serious conversation. You don't want to derail the whole game because you have hit upon something important—that will make the game suspect in the future. So code an answer that may take some time to work through under "come back to this later." And don't press too hard, too often. This game is about helping to create patterns of conversations that are fun, reinforcing, and safe. The aim will be to create a climate where those serious questions can be answered in due time—broach it and wait. The only exception, of course, is anything that bears on your child's safety.

What If I Am Embarrassed by a Question?

Answering hard questions emboldens your child to answer hard questions, too. Children *like* seeing their parents slightly (to greatly) uncomfortable.

They want to see you as someone they can identify with, as well as respect and look up to. That's why I've included so many questions about mistakes or awkward moments (and even about romance and relationships) for them to ask you about. They will play this game for those questions alone.

Remember, the goal here is to talk and get closer. What's a little embarrassment compared to that? Of course, if you really find a question objectionable—select it as one of the two per game you're allowed to skip. But be nice about it. After all, I put it in there, they didn't. Don't blame the messenger. Keep the tone friendly and in the spirit of the game. Happily say, "Ask me that question some other time after I've had a chance to think about it." Or, "I can't answer that now, but I think I can after you get married." Or say "I'm not comfortable with that question right now, but sometime I might be. Let's save that question until *I'm* older." *Whatever*, just so the mood isn't broken.

What If My Child Doesn't Want to Answer a Lot of These Questions?

Well, that tells you something, doesn't it? Look carefully at the ones he or she chooses (even check them) and the ones that are rejected. Even code the ones your child chooses to ask you. You should get some pretty good hints from this about what he or she feels comfortable about and what is threatening. If you think something is wrong, if, for example, he skips any revealing questions about himself, you might float the hypothesis that your child feels insecure and is worried about your opinion. Maybe this would be a good time to go on a reassurance-and-compliments campaign. Or watch and see if you get more open answers after you have been particularly revealing (and pitiful) in your own answer. Don't push to get the answers—analyze. Use the game to create some theories about what your child feels good and bad about and then try, in other circumstances, to address those problems or insecurities. There are enough lighthearted questions in here to keep the game going and at least keep some kind of communication between you.

Why This Book Can Really Help Your Relationship with Your Children

Even if your kids don't talk to you much, they talk to someone. It might be to their friends, to the dog, or to themselves, deep within the privacy of their own mind. They need you to be a part of that conversation. They need your input—and they need to know you—more than as a taskmaster or jovial playmate. All children want to know who their parents "really are" (a lot of grown-up children spend a lot of time on a psychiatrist's couch lamenting that they really never knew their father or, more rarely, their mother). You are finding out about them, and what's just as important, you are letting them find out about you—not in ways that undermine your authority, but in ways that make you more human, and hence, more interesting. So try to answer the questions as honestly as you would with a friend, and let them inside your head and heart. You may inspire the same from them, but even if you don't—and even if you can't measure the impact on them right then—let me assure you that in the long term, these conversations will mean a lot to them. At the very least, the game will slow down the day or evening and create more family time. People will not drift to their own corners of the home in their usual way—and the anticipation of some good questions will promote fun and camaraderie.

What If We Run into Problems and We Have a Bad Experience?

Hey, you've got family, you've got complexity! Everyone can start talking at once. Your daughter may get miffed that her brother took the question she wanted. Two siblings can start fighting over who had the bigger dessert and suddenly you have no cooperation, no goodwill, just one of those nights when you wonder about those lucky people who never settled down. When these unfortunate moments occur, I recommend just putting the book away for that evening and figuring out something else to do. Unless you can quash the insurrection before the kids really get going, it's no use playing this game when everyone has ruffled feathers. The questions will be spit out, the answers will be distorted, and the game will get a bad name. Use the game as a reward rather than as a chore; if people don't act well, save the game until they do. If they really like it, it will be a reinforcement for good behavior—maybe even an inducement. At least you have a shot at this possibility.

But don't worry. Usually no problem will occur. Your family is going to like this enough not to want to mess it up. It will be a good use of your time together and it should have immediate effects on your conversational style and your approach to having conversations. And when you run out of questions, make up some of your own! If you find some great ones, let me know and we'll include them in the next edition of this book. Talk! Listen! And most of all, enjoy each other!

So Where Do We Find the Questions?

Immediately following are the questions for parents to ask kids. On the flip side of the book is the list of questions for kids to ask parents. There is also an introduction there written specifically for the kids.

201 QUESTIONS FOR PARENTS TO ASK KIDS

1.

Tell me the five best things about you.

2.

What does the word "success" mean to you?

3.

Why do kids put rings in their eyebrows and nose?

4.

········

If you could tell me never to serve two vegetables
again, which two would you choose?

5.

········

Who do you think I'd rather you be: an NBA
ballplayer, the mayor, a famous explorer,
or a movie star? Why?

6.

········

Which of your friends do you think I like the most?
Why?

7.

On a scale of one to nine—one being not at all and nine being totally—how strict do you think I am? Where on the scale would you like me to be? (*Parents:* you can draw this on paper to make it easier for smaller children.)

8.

What would be the ideal allowance? Tell me how you would use it.

9.

Who was the worst teacher you ever had? Tell me why.

10.

....

What would the ideal teacher be like?

11.

....

If you had to have one of these, which would you pick—and why? Really long nose hairs, hair in your ears, hair above your lip, massively hairy armpits!

12.

....

How much privacy would you like? What times of the day would you like to be alone, and why?

13.

....

Which of our friends is the funniest looking? Why?

14.

· · · · · · · · · · · · · · · · · · ·

If you could arrange it, what time would I
come home from work? Then, what would
we do together?

15.

· · · · · · · · · · · · · · · · · · ·

Can you think of any clothes that I should
never put on again? Why?

16.

· · · · · · · · · · · · · · · · · · ·

Do you think I drink too much? Have I ever
embarrassed you that way?

17.

....

Which of the following choices do you think
would be best, and why?

a. Dinner with everyone at the table and the TV
on with your favorite program

b. Dinner in which everybody took what they
wanted from the fridge and no one had to
eat the same thing

c. Dinner with the whole family together and no
TV on

18.

....

If a genie would give you only one wish,
which would you pick, and why?

a. being world-class attractive

b. being a genius

c. being famous for doing something great

19.

....

If you are feeling sad, what meal that I could make or order would be the one that would cheer you up?

20.

....

Are you afraid when we fly?

21.

....

Tell me who you think are the three greatest musicians in the world? Why?

22.
. . . .

What punishment have I given that you thought
was really unfair? Why?

23.
. . . .

If you could change three things about yourself,
what would they be?

24.
. . . .

At what age do you think a child ought to be
tried as an adult if he has hurt someone
very badly? Why?

If you could keep your room any way you wanted,
how would it look?

How much money could you use a week? Why?

What kinds of lies do your friends tell
their parents?

28.

· ·

If you had to have a disability, which one of
these would you pick, and why?

a. blindness

b. deafness

c. inability to walk

29.

· ·

What are the qualities that make a good friend?

30.

· ·

Do you think you should be paid for specific
chores? Which ones? And how much do you
think each is worth?

31.

. . . .

What was your favorite toy when you were little?

32.

. . . .

What do you say to comfort yourself when
something scares you (like when a plane is bumpy,
or when you are in a scary place)?

33.

. . . .

What do you think makes a person good-looking?

34.

. . . .

What would you do if you saw a group of guys who
looked like a gang walking toward you?

35.

. . . .

If you could decorate our place, what would
it look like?

36.

. . . .

What do you think of my driving?

37.

....

Looking at your pictures. When do you think you have been the cutest so far?

38.

....

What do you think are the characteristics that make a good parent?

39.

....

Name the three movie stars you most admire.

40.
· · · · · · · · · · · · · · · · · · · ·

Have you ever imitated something you saw
in a movie? What was it?

41.
· · · · · · · · · · · · · · · · · · · ·

Do you think kids ought to get sex education? If
you do, what kinds of things are appropriate?
If you don't, why not?

42.
· · · · · · · · · · · · · · · · · · · ·

Name a TV or movie star that you think is lame.

43.

Do you think it's important to get physical education in school? Why or why not?

44.

Do you think I lose my temper too often? If so, how often?

45.

What do you think is the right amount of hugging and kissing that should go on between kids and their mom? How about kids and their dad?

46.

. . . .

What is the most enjoyable thing our family has
done together in the last three years?

47.

. . . .

Do you think that kids as young as twelve can
fall in love? If not, at what age do you
think that happens?

48.

. . . .

What do you think is beyond the stars?

★ ★ ★ ★ ★

49.

What is the nicest thing a friend has ever done for you?

50.

Why do you, or don't you, like violent movies?

51.

Name two things we should do as a family on the weekend.

52.

How do you think kids are affected by divorce?

53.

....

Do I ever not notice that you are sad?
What signs should I look for?

54.

....

What sport (that you haven't tried) do you think
you would be good at? Why?

55.

....

Who is the meanest kid you know? Why?

56.
....

Do you believe in heaven? If not, why?
If so, what do you think it's like?

57.
....

If you were going to have a weird, unusual pet,
what would it be? Why would you want that pet?

58.
....

If you could look like anyone, who would it be?
Why?

59.

. . . .

Do you think "honesty is always the best policy"?
Why or why not?

60.

. . . .

What have you done, in school or sports or
anywhere, that you are especially proud of?

61.

. . . .

Do you think girls look better with or without
makeup? Why?

62.
....

Do you think it's bad, okay, or good
for guys to cry at movies? Why?

63.
....

Which of your friends are you proudest of? Why?

64.
....

Have you ever had a dream that really scared you?
What was it about?

65.

·······················

Can you describe the most beautiful place you
have ever visited?

66.

·······················

What kinds of things on TV and in movies make
you laugh?

67.

·······················

Tell me about your two favorite movies of all time
and why you like them so much.

68.

How do you describe me to your friends?

69.

Do you feel you are as intelligent as most of your friends? Why or why not?

70.

What is the scariest movie you've ever seen? Why?

71.

Have you ever gotten really lost? If so, tell me about it. How did you feel?

······················

How much TV a day do you think a kid
should watch?

73.

······················

At what age, if any, do you think a kid
should be able to watch any program
no matter what is in it?

74.

······················

Do you think you live in a dangerous
neighborhood? Why or why not?

75.

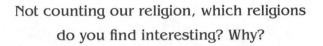

Not counting our religion, which religions
do you find interesting? Why?

76.

Tell me what you think is good, or bad,
about rap music.

77.

Do you ever feel you could lose your temper
so badly that you could hurt someone?
If so, what has made you feel like that?

78.

· ·

What is the grossest thing you can think of?

79.

· ·

Has an adult ever hit you that you haven't
told me about?

80.

· ·

Is there anybody in history that you have read
about that you would like to be?

81.

· ·

What do you think is the right age for marriage?
Why?

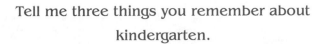

82.
....

Tell me three things you remember about
kindergarten.

83.
....

What kids are popular in your grade? What do
you think makes a person popular?

84.

....

Has anyone ever tried to sell you drugs?
If so, what did you say to that person?

85.

....

If you knew a friend of yours had stolen
something, what would you do about it?

86.

....

Do you feel close to any of your grandparents,
aunts, or uncles? If so, to whom
do you feel closest?

87.

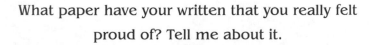

What paper have your written that you really felt
proud of? Tell me about it.

88.

If you could trade lives with somebody
you know, who would it be?

89.

How do you think you would feel if you thought
you were going to be the first person to meet
someone from outer space? What would
you say or ask?

90.

. . . .

What would you do if you were invisible for a day?

91.

. . . .

What is your very earliest memory as a
very little kid?

92.

. . . .

Do you think any of our neighbors are scary?

93.

What would you do if you found out one of your teachers was homosexual?

94.

Is there anything you pretend you understand, but you really don't? What is it?

95.

Who do you think you are most like in our family? Why?

96.
....

Do you believe men and women are equally smart?
Why or why not?

97.
....

Do you ever have a dream that comes back over
and over? If so, what is it like?

98.
....

Why do you think some people don't like animals?

99.

. . . .

What kind of person should be
President of the United States?

100.

. . . .

Why are sports so important to kids?

101.

. . . .

Which of your friend's parents do you like
being around the most? Why?

102.

Have you ever done something that you
realized later could have really been
dangerous? What was it?

103.

Do you think people ought to be able to
carry guns? Why or why not?

104.

Do you feel they ought to teach about religion
in schools? Why or why not?

105.
....

Have you ever looked at some of the X-rated sites
on the Internet? If so, what did you see and
what did you think of it?

106.
....

Under what circumstances do you think it is right
to tell an adult that a friend of yours has
done something really bad?

107.
....

If you had bad breath, would you want someone
to tell you about it? How would you react?

108.
....

What would you do if you saw an adult kick a dog?

109.
....

Did you ever have a close friend betray a really
important confidence? How did you handle it?

110.
....

How do you determine which of your
clothes are dirty?

111.
....

What do you purposely do to tick me off?

112.
....

What do you think is the right age to have children?
Why?

113.
....

What is your favorite joke?

114.
....

What is the best toy I ever gave you?

115.
....

What person is your favorite hero—real
or made-up?

116.
....

When you hear about kids bringing guns to school and shooting kids and adults, does it seem like something that could happen at your school? Why or why not?

117.
....

What do I do that embarrasses you?

118.
....

Tell me about a time I said "no" in a way that made you want to go right out and disobey me!

119.

What is your favorite part of cartoons?

120.

Why do you think people use illegal drugs?

121.

What is your favorite fairy tale? Why?

122.

If someone you didn't like wanted to be your
friend, how would you handle the situation?

123.
. . . .

Have you—or has anyone you know—ever thought
about suicide? Tell me about it.

124.
. . . .

Do you remember any single piece of clothing from
when you were younger that you really loved?
What made it special?

125.
. . . .

Do you tell me when you aren't feeling well?
If not, why not?

126.

. . . .

Do you think that kids ought to be able to see any
movie they want, or that it's good that there are
some movies you have to be eighteen to see?
Why or why not?

127.

. . . .

What would be the ideal number of hours for our
family to be together every day?

128.
....

How often do you think your parents fight?
What do we fight about?

129.
....

If you could conduct an assembly at your school
and talk about anything you wanted to, what
would be the subject of your speech?
Why?

130.
....

Under what circumstances, if any, is divorce okay?
Why?

131.
....

If you could design a full day of television programs, what kind of programs would you pick?

132.
....

How often do I have bad breath?

133.
....

Is there some part of your body you worry about?

134.
....

What do you think causes prejudice?

135.
....

Do you think it matters who is President of the United States? Why or why not?

136.
....

Do you think a child should ever be taken away from his or her parents permanently? Tell me why you think the way you do.

137.
....

Who do you think has a harder life, kids or adults? Why?

138.

Why do people give to charity? How much
should people give?

139.

Why do you think people drink alcohol?
What do you think about that?

140.

If your best friend took a weapon to school,
would you tell on him?
Why or why not?

141.
....

How attractive do you think you are?

142.
....

What would you do if I fainted and didn't
get back up right away?

143.
....

When you watch natural disasters on TV, like
floods, hurricanes, or earthquakes, do you think
it could happen to us? What do you think about
when you see bad things happen to people on TV?

144.
....

What makes a person someone you want to know?

145.
....

If I weren't here and you had to choose one of
my friends to replace me as your parent,
who would it be?

146.
....

What have you done in school that you are most
proud of—no matter what kind of grade you
got on it?

147.

If you could go on a trip with your two best friends, where would you go?

148.

If you couldn't live in the United States, what other country would you pick?

149.

How do you feel about people when they are very overweight? Why?

150.

....

What's the best surprise you ever had? What's the best surprise you would order up if you could?

151.

....

Let's say the kids in your school had to take it over for a week, and you had to teach one of the classes. Which one would you pick? What kinds of things would you do in class?

152.

....

What is the most precious thing you own? Why?

153.
....

Are there any limits to what a friend should do for
a friend? Why or why not? If there are limits,
what should they be?

154.
....

Do you think we trust you enough, or too much?
Why?

155.
....

If I could grant you one wish that would only be
true for twenty-four hours, what would it be?

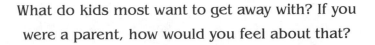

156.

. . . .

What do kids most want to get away with? If you
were a parent, how would you feel about that?

157.

. . . .

What desserts are overrated?

158.

. . . .

How strong (physically) do you think you are? Why?

159.
....

What have you been taught about AIDS? Why do you think they should or should not teach about AIDS in school?

160.
....

What is the earliest memory that you have?

161.
....

Do you think it is okay for girls to be taller than boys? Why or why not?

162.
....

What would you do if you were lost in a forest?

163.
....

Do you ever talk to God? If you do, what kinds
of things do you talk about?

164.
....

What situation would you rather be in and why?
  a. You are the only boy in an all-girls school (or
     the only girl in an all-boys school)
  b. You are the only person of your race on an
     island
  c. You are the only kid in a country of grown-
     ups

165.
....

If you could change one thing about your body—
face, weight, anything—what would you change?

166.

....

What do you think is the most common parental mistake: too much attention to their teenager, or too little attention to their teenager? Why?

167.

....

Out of ages five to one hundred, what do you think is the best age to be? Why?

168.

....

When are you happiest? Why?

169.

· ·

What makes you respect a teacher or coach?
What loses your respect?

170.

· ·

If we could have three dogs and you could pick
them all, which breeds would you choose?

171.

· ·

What are the worst chores we ask you to do?

172.

· ·

Why do you think I married your father/mother?

173.

· ·

What do you think is the ideal weight for an average male and female teen? What would be too thin? What would be too fat?

174.

· ·

What is the scariest thing that has ever happened to you?

175.
....

At what age do you think "old age" begins? Why?

176.
....

What do they teach you about your body in school?

177.
....

What have you learned in the last couple days in school that surprised you?

178.

· · · · · · · · · · · · · · · · · · · ·

Pretend that I'm a five-year-old. What are the
most important things that I should know
so that I can be safe?

179.

· · · · · · · · · · · · · · · · · · · ·

How do boys/girls decide who is popular? How
important is it to be considered popular?

180.

· · · · · · · · · · · · · · · · · · · ·

If you could change anything about this family,
what would it be?

181.

Do you think I am conservative about sex?
Why or why not?

182.

Which would you chose: being the smartest kid
you know, being the best athlete in your class,
or being the richest kid in your grade? Why?

183.

Who do you think are the greatest sports stars
who have ever lived?

184.

....

What do you think when you see someone
in a wheelchair?

185.

....

Do you believe in life on other planets?
Why or why not?

186.

....

If you could model yourself after one person,
besides anyone in the family, who would it be?

187.
....

Do you think boys are nicer than girls, or are girls nicer than boys? Or is there no difference?

188.
....

If you were Bill Gates, the richest person in the world, what would you do with your money?

189.
....

If I could be a famous person who is alive now and still be your parent, what famous person would you like me to be?

190.

....

Do you think both men and women should work
when they get married? Should the woman stay
home when there is a small baby, or should
the parents take turns? Why?

191.

....

Did you think the baby-sitters we got for you were
good people or were there any whom you really
disliked? Who were the best and worst? Why?

192.

Do you ever think about me dying? If you do,
what do you think about?

193.
....

Who do you think is the most beautiful actress
in the world? Why?

194.
....

Who is the most recent male heartthrob in the
movies? Why do you think so many
people think he is so great?

195.
....

What is your opinion about sex before marriage?
Do you think it creates problems?

196.
....

What name would you give me if you could name me just like I named you? Why?

197.
....

If you could be any height, what would it be and why?

198.
....

What do you think would make a great trip to take with just you and me, if we could?

199.

·····················

Have you ever had a near miss in a really
dangerous situation? If so, describe it.

200.

·····················

Do you want to have children when you grow up?
Why or why not?

201.

·····················

What do I do that most clearly tells you
that I love you?

199.

Can you love more than one person at the same time?

200.

Were you close with your brother(s)/sister(s) growing up? Were there periods when you didn't like each other? Are you equally close to all your brothers and sisters now? Why or why not?

201.

What are the things I do that you think I get from Dad's side of the family? What are the things I do that you think I get from your side of the family? What things do I do that you can't imagine where they came from?

195.

What would life be like if we were really poor?

196.

What are the things that you like or dislike in my friends?

197.

Do you ever pretend to like someone you really don't like? Why or why not?

198.

Do you believe in miracles? Why or why not?

191.

_ _ ._ ._ ._ ._

What has been your favorite age so far?

192.

_ _ ._ ._ ._ ._

Give me three examples that stand out in your mind
of great times that you and I have had together.

193.

_ _ ._ ._ ._ ._

Tell me about each President you voted for. Why did
you vote for that person? Did you ever regret your vote?

194.

_ _ ._ ._ ._ ._

Who was the first boy/girl you ever fell in love with?

187.

If you had to have a tattoo, what would it be?
Where would it be?

188.

What have you said or done to me that you have
really regretted?

189.

When you are gone, what are the two things that you
would want me to remember most about you?

190.

Have you ever been so angry with someone that you
wished he or she were dead? Why? Did you
continue to feel that way?

184.

Why did you stop with the number of children you have now? Have you ever seriously thought of having another child?

185.

Is there anyone you have lost track of from when you were younger who you would like to find again? Who is this person and why would you like to see him or her again?

186.

What are the three things that you are most thankful for? Why?

181.

— . — . — . — . —

Could you describe what your first bedroom looked
like? Did you feel safe and happy there?
If not, why not?

182.

— . — . — . — . —

What do you think is the right age for kids to
be able to date? Why?

183.

— . — . — . — . —

How would you feel if I requested birth control
information from a health clinic?

178.

What do you think is the meaning of the word "success?" What are the personality traits that are likely to make someone "a success."

179.

If you had known that there was something very wrong with your baby when you were pregnant, would you have considered an abortion? Why or why not?

180.

Have you ever been cheated by someone? What did you do?

175.

Do you think life is more dangerous now than when you were a kid? Why or why not?

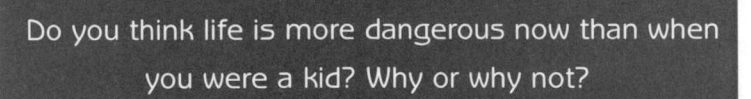

176.

What is the oldest precious object that you have from your family?

177.

Do you think we would ever move/move again? Why or why not?

172.

— · —— · —— · —

Is it important to you that I get married someday?
Why or why not?

173.

— · —— · —— · —

What would your life be like if you had never had children?

174.

— · —— · —— · —

Have you ever gone to see a psychologist or
therapist? If you have, why did you go? Did it help
you? If you didn't, do we know people who have?
Did it help them?

169.

Are there any jobs you have done that you feel bad about doing and wouldn't want me to do? If so, why?

170.

Why do most adult parties have alcohol at them if alcohol is so bad? Is alcohol bad?

171.

When do you think it is important to be able to defend yourself physically?

166.

What is the biggest change from your generation
to mine?

167.

Why do some kids develop eating disorders?

168.

Did you ever feel that you were supposed to get
something good and somebody else got it who
didn't deserve it? If you did, what was it?
If somebody else got it and she did
deserve it more, why did she
deserve it more than you?

163.

Do you think there should be a Take Our Sons to Work Day, just like the Take Our Daughters to Work Day? Why or why not?

164.

Do you think there are any ways that you treat boys and girls differently? If there are, what are they? Why do you feel that way?

165.

Do you think boys and men can kiss and hug as friends like girls and women do? Why or why not?

160.

In high school, were you ever in the arts—painting, drama, or music? Did you ever consider doing it for a career? Why or why not?

161.

Tell me about a couple of events in your life that you think changed your life.

162.

When you were a kid, what were your summers like before you began to work?

157.

How would you feel if I grew up to be more or less religious than you?

158.

Would you ever want to go on an adventure like a safari or sail a boat around the world? Why or why not?

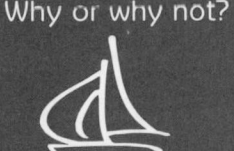

159.

Have you ever come close to death? Did you ever think you were in great danger? What did it feel like?

154.

Did you have zits when you were a teenager?
If you did, did they affect your social life?

155.

Were you good at keeping secrets? Did your friends
confide in you? Did you ever have a secret when you
were young that you told and later felt sorry?

156.

What was your favorite vacation with your parents?

151.

When was the first time you got to use your father's car? What kind of car was it? Did you ever have an accident with it?

152.

Do you believe masturbation is normal and healthy? Why or why not?

153.

What kinds of things do you want me to tell you about my life and what do you think is okay for me to keep private?

147.

— · — · — · — · —

Who was your first date? Did you go out again?
Did you kiss?

148.

— · — · — · — · —

What is the one thing that your parents did for you
that you have tried to pass on to me?

149.

— · — · — · — · —

Do you think boys have to be tougher than girls?
Why or why not?

150.

— · — · — · — · —

If you had a child who turned out to be gay, could
you handle that?

 144.

Have you changed any of your ideas about religion since you were a kid?

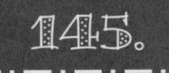 145.

Is there any kind of war that could happen that you would want *me* to join the military to fight against?

146.

Is there anything you ever lost that you still think about?

140.
_ . _ . _ . _ . _

How do you decide who to invite to a party?

141.
_ . _ . _ . _ . _

If you could be any sports hero in the history of
the world, who would it be?

142.
_ . _ . _ . _ . _

Who do you think I look most like in the family? Why?

143.
_ . _ . _ . _ . _

When do you think someone is too old to sleep
with stuffed animals? Why?

136.
_ . _ . _ . _ . _

Were you talented in sports when you were younger?
Whether you were or were not, was it
important to you?

137.
_ . _ . _ . _ . _

Did you turn out the way your parents wanted you to?

138.
_ . _ . _ . _ . _

Who were the five most important people in your life,
not counting any of us or your mom and dad?

139.
_ . _ . _ . _ . _

Do you think a kid's room should be private and
off-limits to adults? Why or why not?

133.

— · — · — · — · —

Do you ever daydream? If you do, what stories do you make up in your head—or do you have a really favorite dream that you think about?

134.

— · — · — · — · —

Do you think I talk back to you too often? How does it make you feel? Why does it bother you so much?

135.

— · — · — · — · —

If you could be one of the characters in *Star Trek*, which one would you be and why?

130.

Did both your parents and Mom's/Dad's parents approve of your marriage? Why or why not?

131.

What kinds of things make you lose your temper the easiest?

132.

Has there been any time when you were exceptionally proud of me? When was it and why was it special?

127.

_ . _ . _ . _ . _

Why do some fathers stop paying child support after
a divorce? Does that mean they never really
loved the children?

128.

_ . _ . _ . _ . _

Why are parents always worried about how their kid is
dressed? Why don't they trust the kid to have his or
her own taste, or to know how warm or cold he
or she wants to be?

129.

_ . _ . _ . _ . _

How long do you want to live? Why?

124.

Do you think I am appreciative enough?
Why or why not?

125.

Did you ever give something up—a sport or an
instrument, for example—that you wished you
hadn't? Do you ever think of going back to it?

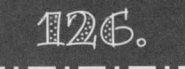

126.

Why do adults get so upset when a kid swears,
when *they* do it all the time?

120.

How do you think mothers and fathers are different?

121.

_ . _ . _ . _ . _

Were you ever the victim of racism or sexism?
Tell me what happened.

122.

Do you think politicians are honest or not? Why?
What kinds of people should run for office?

123.

_ . _ . _ . _ . _

Did you and Mom/Dad ever have such a bad
argument that you thought about breaking up?

117.

Tell me about something that *you* were really proud of when you were in college or when you first started working. What did you tell your parents that made *them* proud of you?

118.

Some people teach their kids how to shoot guns. Do you feel this is good or bad? Why?

119.

Did I have any really annoying habits when I was a very little baby or young kid? Did I have any adorable ones?

114.

— · — · — · — · —

If you were going to describe me to one of your
friends and could only use three words,
what would they be?

115.

— · — · — · — · —

Name your three best friends. Why are you closest
to these people? What makes someone worth
being a best friend?

116.

— · — · — · — · —

What did you do as a kid that you tell me not to do?
Why do you tell me not to do it?

111.

What would happen if something happened to you?
Who would take care of me?
Would I have any choice?

112.

Were you ever a hippie or a preppie
when you were growing up?

113.

Why do you think there's so much divorce
these days?

108.

When you fought with your parents, did you
make up fast or did it last a long time?

109.

Do you think smoking is as bad as drugs?
Why or why not?

110.

Why do you think people should save their money?
Are you saving a lot of money?

104.

What do you think the world will be like when
I am your age?

105.

Did you have any problems learning a subject when
you were in middle school? High school?

106.

Some people say that high school was the best time
of their lives. Was it for you? If it wasn't, what was?

107.

How do you know when you are really in love?

101.

— · — · — · — · —

Has there been a time since I've been alive that
you've cried and I wasn't aware of it? Could
you tell me what it was about?

102.

— · — · — · — · —

What aspect of your childhood would you like me
to have? What aspect of your childhood would
you like me to avoid?

103.

— · — · — · — · —

Did you ever try any kind of drugs?
Why or why not?

98.
— · —· · —· · — · —

When you were young, did you collect anything?
If you did, what was it and why
did you get into that?

99.
— · —· · —· · — · —

When you were in high school, what did you want to
be when you grew up? What about in college?
How did you come up with those ideas?

100.
— · —· · —· · — · —

Who was more strict when you were growing up,
your mother or father? How did you
feel about that?

95.

What special kinds of food did your mother give you when you were sick? Why did she give you those foods?

96.

Why do some people think it's important for husbands and wives to have the same religion?

97.

What makes a TV program good, or bad, for kids?

92.

Did you have a nickname in middle school or high school? If so, what was it and how did you get it?

93.

When you were a kid, did you have a favorite hiding place? If you did, where was it and what did you do there?

94.

When you were a kid, did you ever belong to a club? If you did, how did people become a member and what did you do together?

89.
— · — · — · — · —

What were the three happiest moments in your
life so far?

90.
— · — · — · — · —

What things do we have now that you didn't have
when you were growing up?

91.
— · — · — · — · —

What kinds of things did your mom and dad do with
you that you have tried to do differently with us?

86.

If you could look like any movie star, who would it be?
Why?

87.

Who was the best teacher you ever had? And
the worst? Why?

88.

What toy did you want when you were a kid that
you never got?

82.

In what ways do you think you are similar to me?

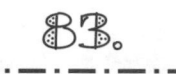
83.

In what ways do you think you are different from me?

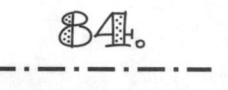
84.

What was your biggest disappointment when you were a kid?

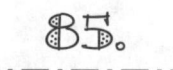
85.

What is the thing you wanted most that you haven't gotten?

78.

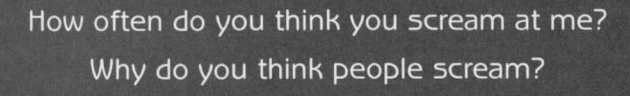

How often do you think you scream at me?
Why do you think people scream?

79.

How would you feel if I changed my first name?
Last name?

80.

What really gives you the creeps?

81.

How did you like middle school? High school?
Why or why not?

75.

Is my personality the same now as it was when
I was younger? Tell me how I am the
same or different.

76.

Why is it such a big deal for rooms to be clean?

77.

Why do you care if I fight with my brothers or sisters
or wrestle with my friends?

71.

Have you ever thought of adopting a child?
Why or why not?

72.

What did you get in trouble for when you were a kid?

73.

Did you ever have a teacher who picked on you?

74.

What was the most embarrassing thing that
ever happened to you?

68.

Why do women shave their armpits and men don't?

69.

If you won the lottery, what would you do with the money?

70.

What makes you like one of my friends? What would make you dislike one of my friends?

65.

Would you admit to me if you were afraid of something?

66.

Do you think there should be a death penalty for murder, or should the worst possible punishment be life in prison? Tell me why you have this opinion.

67.

Do you think it is okay for a man to be the person who stays home with kids instead of the woman? Why or why not?

61.
— · — · — · — · —

If you could be any female sports star,
who would you be?

62.
— · — · — · — · —

Do you believe men and women ought to be equal
partners, or should the man be in charge? Why? Did
you and Mom/Dad talk about this before marriage?

63.
— · — · — · — · —

Did you ever get jealous of someone?

64.
— · — · — · — · —

Do you think people are born intelligent, or can
they be made intelligent?

57.

There are two kinds of weddings: big fancy ones and small private ones. Which do you like?

58.

Did you ever run away from home? If you did, why did you do it? If you didn't, did you ever think about it? Do you remember what the issue was?

59.

What are your all-time favorite movies? Why?

60.

What kinds of things make you sad?

54.

Did kids ever make fun of you for any reason?
What do you remember best?

55.

When you were younger, did you ever drink too much
and get sick? If so, how did that happen?

56.

Would you get upset if I wanted to live in another
country when I was grown up? Why or why not?

51.

What age group of kids do you think you are best with: babies, middle school, or high school?

52.

Over your lifetime there have been a lot of different kinds of music. What is your all-time favorite? Why?

53.

What have you said to me that you wish you hadn't?

48.

What is the worst thing that your parents ever said to you?

49.

Did you want a marriage like the one your parents had? Why or why not?

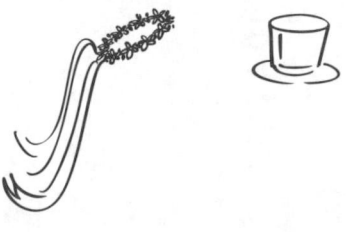

50.

What makes you lose your temper with me?

44.

Would you rather be famous, or make a lot of money? Why?

45.

When you are really old, would you want to live with me, in a community for elderly people, or in your own place? Tell me why.

46.

What is your opinion of nude scenes in movies?

47.

Have you ever been hit? If so, tell me what happened.

41.

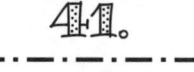

How much money does a person need
to have a good life?

42.

Did you ever wish you didn't have children?
If so, what made you think that?

43.

If you could do only one of the following, which do
you think is the best use of money: being able to
take family vacations, having a really nice home, or
being able to send your children to a great college?
Why?

37.

What do you think is your worst bad habit?

38.

Have you ever done something brave?
If so, did you regret it?

39.

What's the worst dream you can remember?

40.

How many times have you been in love?

33.

How would you describe Dad/Mom the first
time you saw him/her?

34.
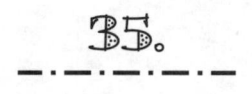

If there were a war against the United States, how
would you feel about volunteering for duty?

35.

What makes a good friend?

36.

How do you tell when someone is lying?

30.

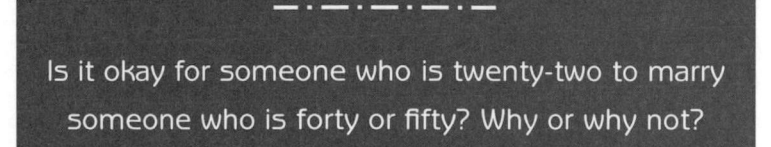

Is it okay for someone who is twenty-two to marry someone who is forty or fifty? Why or why not?

31.

How would people who knew you in middle school describe you then?

32.

How would people who knew you in high school describe you?

27.

Is there any experience that you have not had that you regret not having?

28.

What qualities do you most respect in a woman? In a man?

29.

Do you think we should know details of political people's private lives, like the President of the United States?

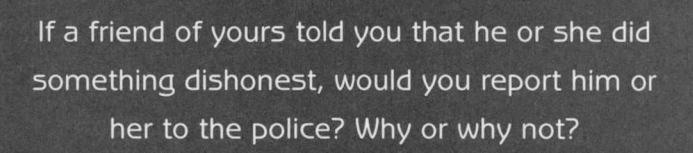

24.

If a friend of yours told you that he or she did something dishonest, would you report him or her to the police? Why or why not?

25.

How important do you think it is to look really good?

26.

What kinds of scenes in movies make you cry?

20.

— · — · — · — · —

What was the best thing I ever gave you?

21.
— · — · — · — · —

Who was your best friend in high school and what was the best thing about this person?

22.

— · — · — · — · —

If you could afford any car in the world, what would it be?

23.
— · — · — · — · —

Do you think you have any prejudices?
What would they be?

17.

_·_·_·_·_·_

What was your favorite pet when you were a kid?

18.

_·_·_·_·_·_

Why did your parents give you your name?

19.

_·_·_·_·_·_

What is your favorite joke? Why?

13.
— . — . — . — . —

How old do you think you look? Why?

14.
— . — . — . — . —

When did you have your first kiss? Who did
you have it with? Did you like it?

15.
— . — . — . — . —

How did you and Mom/Dad meet?

16.
— . — . — . — . —

How old are you in your dreams?
What are you doing?

9.

What was your most important relationship in high school and why did it end?

10.

If you could do any job in the world, besides the one you are doing now, what would it be?

11.

What kinds of things get you the angriest? Why?

12.

When, if ever, do you think it's okay to tell a lie?

6.
— · — · — · — · —

Did you have big fights with your mom when you were growing up? If so, what were they usually about?

7.
— · — · — · — · —

Did you have big fights with your dad when you were growing up? If so, what were they usually about?

8.
— · — · — · — · —

Did you ever get arrested for anything? If not, did you ever do anything you should have gotten in trouble for if anyone had found out?

3.
— · — · — · — · — ·

What was your first car? What was your favorite car when you were young?

4.
— · — · — · — · — ·

How often do you go over the speed limit?

5.
— · — · — · — · — ·

Were you considered popular in middle school or high school? Why or why not?

201 QUESTIONS FOR KIDS TO ASK PARENTS

1.

— · — · — · — · —

When you were young, were you involved in any kind of political protests such as for the Civil Rights movement or against Vietnam? Why or why not?

2.

— · — · — · — · —

What tells you when a child is responsible enough to trust a lot?

another edition of *201 Questions*, we may use your ideas!)

Well, I guess that's it. As they say in the Olympics—*Let the games begin!*

that everyone gets to join in. That's part of the fun. See what they say and then put your own contribution into the mix!

So Don't Worry . . .

I don't promise too much too often, but I promise you that if you play this game with an open mind, you are going to enjoy it. I know you will learn things about the people you play with that you didn't know when you started. And I promise you one big surprise: *You will also learn things about yourself that you didn't know before.* You may even enjoy this game so much that you add some variations—like everyone concentrating on a single subject area (sports experiences, for example) and doing a round of questions that people make up themselves. I think that would be great—but wait until you've played with my questions for awhile so that you get in sync with the spirit of the game. (On the other hand, if you do make up great questions, pass them on to me care of Avon Books, the publisher of this book, in New York. If we do

you have to remind each other that everyone has the
right to his opinion in this game.

. . . *I can't think of anything to say!* This happens a lot
less than you might imagine. But if it does happen,
just ask for another question. It's no big deal, and you
do want to talk about something that interests you.
The question you skipped can be asked again some
other time, and by then you may have thought about
some way you'd like to answer it.

. . . *I don't want to answer that question.* Remember:
Everyone gets to skip two questions. You don't have
to give a reason why. Just say "Next question,
please!" No one is supposed to pressure anyone.
Remember this theme: This is supposed to be fun,
and we all have to make sure that we keep it fun!

. . . *I'd like to answer somebody else's question.* You
can get a chance to do that in the group discussion
that follows that person's answer. The person who ini-
tially gets asked the question gets all the time he or
she wants to think about it and talk about it. But after

Start modestly the first time. Don't let the game go on so long that it gets tiresome. A half hour is a good amount of time to try first, see if that is too long or too short. Decide on a good place for your family to begin: in the living room, on a trip, or at the dinner table. Try alternating questions that are funny and ones that might be a little tough to answer because they are very personal. Be honest and remember (this is always hard to do) that parents are people, too, and they don't want to be hit with a string of "hot questions" any more than you do.

What If . . .

. . . *my parents criticize something I say.* Tell them that they can't do that in this game. Criticism stifles conversation. If your three favorite foods are chocolate, popcorn, and Fritos, so be it! In this game, they have to respect that. Now it is fair to ask if you are sure you want to choose those three to be the only things you would exist on forever. You might want to revise your choices . . . but they are *your* choices and

This isn't hard—you are just taking turns and not letting anyone hog airtime. And all the rules are simple:

- You take your questions from the list that follows this introduction (even if you are a teenager and the word "kid" is a major insult—sorry!)

- No one interrupts anyone else.

- You (and anyone else) can only refuse to answer two questions during any game.

- Show no disrespect (grimacing, eye rolling, cutting remarks, etc). This one is a very hard rule for brothers and sisters to follow, but try.

- The person who asks the question gets to ask a follow-up question if it directly relates to the answer.

- Use sensitivity when choosing questions: if you know that a specific question is going to be upsetting because of some recent event or loss, skip it.

Remember, the point of this game is *fun*.

How to Play

Decide how long you are going to play. One turn apiece? That means everyone gets asked one question and then you stop. That seems too short, doesn't it? Well, maybe, three turns a piece? Half an hour? It's a personal decision, but you probably should get to ask and answer at least a few questions.

Once you decide how long you will play, decide the order in which you will go. Flip a coin to see who goes first, second, third, etc. Alternate between adults and children if possible. For example, a parent starts and picks a question for the kid who comes next and that kid asks a question of the next adult.

The person asking the question can pick any question out of his section of the book (parents ask parent questions, kids ask kid questions), *but* they have to pick it quickly—no pouring through the book for what could seem like hours! The person who answers can answer briefly—or take up to five minutes. Then the question is open for discussion to everyone—if anyone has more to say on the subject! People can take as long as they like unless you make a rule that no question gets more than a certain amount of time for group discussion.

kind of house you would pick if it was up to you—but you will find out something about what you really like when you have to state a preference.)

When your parents pick a question and ask you to answer it, you might worry that it will be too tough a request. But it won't be. This book will not put you in too ticklish a spot. Absolutely not. The point of this book is to discover each other in a good way . . . and have fun doing it. Did you know that sometimes kids grow up and never find out who was the first person their mother dated or what their father's all-time favorite songs were? I can't let that happen to you. This book is based on the premise that the more you know about your family members, the closer you all are; some things you say will be funny and others will just be revealing and thoughtful. I guarantee you, though, once you start picking questions and taking turns giving answers, you will want to keep playing—because there will be so many interesting things to think about or give your opinion about that you won't want to stop.

The trick of good family conversation is that questions have to be really worth asking and answering. So I have taken a lot of care about which questions to include in this book. In fact, I went to the experts. I sat down with my kids and asked them to help me think of questions that wouldn't be boring, too embarrassing, dumb, or demanding. I liked most of the questions they came up with. But I needed even more questions. So I went out and asked a lot of other people— both parents and kids—what subjects and what stories about each other they would really like to know about.

The questions in this book are the result of that search. I think that if you ask your parents some of these questions, you will get to see them in ways you've never seen them before. I also think there are questions here that they can ask you that will give you a chance to shine: to be funny, truthful, and smart. Most of these questions will also make you think about what is important to you or your parents. You can find out about the experiences and feelings in your parents' lives—and in your own life—that made everyone who they are today. (For example, you might not have really thought about what movie star you would most like to look like [and why] or what

with them. They'll learn a lot about what you think are ways kids act nasty!

You can wiggle out of any two questions that don't interest you or are embarrassing—but no more than that. It's good if a question makes you squirm a little; that means you either haven't thought about it before, or you have but you haven't wanted to deal with it. But why not try out an answer? Pick a set length of time to play for—and my guess is you'll want to extend it. These questions get addictive! You can play them at the dinner table, or after dinner, or on a car trip, or anytime you feel like hearing what your parents will say about something.

So, this is a book about how to have interesting and often funny conversations with your family. It's a way to avoid dead, boring silences and fill the time instead with questions and answers that everyone will enjoy thinking about. I know that in my family, it is too easy for us to get stuck talking about practical things like who has to be taken where the next day. That isn't particularly fun. It doesn't let me in on what my kids are thinking, and it doesn't help my two teenagers learn things that might help them understand me a little better.

imagine what life would be like if we could design it any way we wanted. In fact, I wrote this book because I think talking can be terrific fun, and even talking to your parents and brothers or sisters can be a kind of great game. Everyone can get to know each other and laugh a lot—and be amazed from time to time. No one wins or loses, but there is an element of surprise in finding out personal information about parents— and sharing some of your ideas, daydreams, and opinions with them.

My idea is to think of some of the world's most interesting questions that parents and kids could talk about and give everyone the chance to pick the ones they'd like to hear about. Each person picks a question to ask and then answers a question when his or her turn comes around. All you have to do is choose from the list under *201 Questions to Ask Your Parents* and ask any question you want. Your parents can take as long or as short a time as they want to answer. And you can all discuss the topic if you like. But then they go into their section of the book and ask *you* questions. Some of them might not be so interesting, but others—like asking you who is the meanest kid you know—might be cool to think about and share

AN INTRODUCTION FOR KIDS

Wouldn't it be fun to find out more about what your father or mother was like when he or she was a kid? Or get to tell your parents which of their friends you think looks dorkiest? Wouldn't conversation be more interesting if you and your family traded unexpected questions and answers at dinner rather than just talked about what homework did or didn't get done?

There are a lot of great things to talk about that no one ever brings up because we usually think of conversation as being serious rather than a way of being playful. Of course, conversation should be about serious things some of the time—some of the questions in this book are about very serious topics. But other times, questions should be asked just to create new ways to think about things, look back on our lives, or

201

Questions
to Ask Your
Parents

Pepper Schwartz, Ph.D.

AVON BOOKS  NEW YORK